BETWEEN
BROTHERS & SISTERS

Avon Books are available at special quantity discounts for bulk purchases for sales promotions, premiums, fund raising or educational use. Special books, or book excerpts, can also be created to fit specific needs.

For details write or telephone the office of the Director of Special Markets, Avon Books, Dept. FP, 1350 Avenue of the Americas, New York, New York 10019, 1-800-238-0658.

BETWEEN BROTHERS & SISTERS

A Celebration of Life's Most Enduring Relationship

ADELE FABER and ELAINE MAZLISH

Developed by the Philip Lief Group, Inc.

AVON BOOKS  NEW YORK

AVON BOOKS
A division of
The Hearst Corporation
1350 Avenue of the Americas
New York, New York 10019

The G.P. Putnam's Sons edition contains the following Library of Congress Cataloging in Publication Data:

Faber, Adele.
    Between brothers and sisters: a celebration of life's most enduring realtionship/by Adele Faber and Elaine Mazlish; developed by the Philip Lief Group; photo research by Fay Torresyap; designed by Joe Marc Freedman.
        p.   cm.
1. Brothers and sisters—Poetry. 2. Brothers and sisters—
Portraits. I. Mazlish, Elaine. II. Philip Lief Group.
III. Title.
PS3556.A16B4   1989   89-36294 CIP
811'.54—dc20

First Avon Books Trade Printing: April 1991

AVON TRADEMARK REG. U.S. PAT. OFF. AND IN OTHER COUNTRIES, MARCA REGISTRADA, HECHO EN U.S.A.

Printed in the U.S.A.

ARC   10 9 8 7 6 5 4

We Thank You

A small number of people were vital to the evolution of this book:

Kevin Osborn came up with the original idea for it, and Philip Lief, the producer, gave us his unflagging support during the long photo selection process.

Bob Markel contributed his keen aesthetic sensibilities and his years of experience as publisher and editor of many distinguished "picture books."

Our friends at *Mothering* magazine sent us what must have been their entire picture file on siblings along with several pages listing the names and addresses of their best photographers. All proved invaluable.

Fay Torresyap, our photo researcher, was extraordinarily sensitive to our needs and persistent in her efforts to track down the specific photographs we requested.

Judy Linden, our editor, alternately cheered us on and reined us in. Her enthusiasm kept our spirits high and her insistence upon sparseness ("Do we really need five pictures of siblings on swings—no matter how enchanting?") has led to a livelier book.

Joe Freedman, our interior designer, placed and juxtaposed our pictures in ways that were true to our intentions.

Our husbands, Robert Mazlish and Leslie Faber, after a full day of their own work, came home each night and gave "quality time" to our work. Their thoughtful and perceptive comments influenced many of our decisions.

Finally we wish to thank all the photographers who sent us the products of their passion. It is through the eyes of these artists that we have been able to express our vision.

Behind the Scenes

Each of our first three books was a labor of love, born of our deepest convictions. *Between Brothers and Sisters* was an unplanned child.

It began with a phone call from Bob Markel, our agent and good friend. How would we feel about writing an introduction for a book of photographs about siblings? We were not enthusiastic. Why would we do it? What could we say that wouldn't be a repetition of what we had already written in *Siblings Without Rivalry?* Besides, we had spent the last five years talking, thinking, sleeping, breathing "siblings" and we were ready to move on.

Bob hastened to assure us that very little work would be involved.

"How little?"

"A few days. Maybe a week at the most."

Still we hesitated.

Would we at least come up to the office of the producer of the proposed book and look at the photographs?

Yes, we would.

The following Friday we met at Philip Lief's office. After introductions and a few pleasantries, we were led to a desk heaped high with stacks of photo copies of pictures of siblings of every size, shape, color, and nationality. We sat side by side, sifting through the piles, exclaiming to each other, mesmerized by what these gray and fuzzy prints revealed. *The sibling experience was universal!* We had known it intellectually, but now we were seeing it in all its fascinating, cultural diversity, each telling moment frozen in time, caught by the click of a shutter:

A young black child in a New York City playground, saddled with a baby in her arms, while her friends are free to play.

A little Guatemalan girl carrying a child on her back that's almost as big as she is.

A young girl from Nepal washing her brother's bottom at a public pump.

A Chinese boy feeding his little brother with chopsticks.

Before we knew it, we had separated these pictures into an "older sibs as caretakers" pile. Then we went on sorting, commenting, categorizing. There were the "angry pictures," teeth bared, eyes blazing. And the pictures of sisters and brothers tenderly comforting each other. And the photographs of older siblings, like the work-worn sisters from Appalachia whose bond was written in the deep lines of their faces. Slowly the whole sibling saga began to take shape: the intensity of the feelings and the ambivalence—the love and the hatred, the irritation and the pleasure, the meaning of being a sibling from the moment of birth to the final years of life.

We were overwhelmed by the beauty and significance of the raw material in our hands. Yes, we would do an introduction, but we could never stop there. It would have to be *our* book, the pictures *we* chose, the statement about "siblingship" *we* wanted to make. Yes, we would use some of these photographs, but for the larger vision that was already beginning to form in our minds, we would need many more pictures to choose from. Philip and Bob offered full support for what had suddenly become our project.

We took the photo copies home, studied them, and made long lists of what we still needed. Philip put us in touch with a gifted young photo researcher, Fay Torresyap, who came out to Long Island to see what we already had and to listen to us describe what we felt was still missing. Over the next few months the Federal Express driver, bearing boxes of pictures from dozens of photographers, became a familiar sight in our driveways.

As we selected, assembled, and reassembled the pictures, we saw that we could not do justice to the tale that was unfolding before us with ordinary prose. We tried. The words wouldn't come. Each photograph was a poem and cried out for poetic commentary. That realization was our breakthrough. Once we allowed ourselves the freedom and the rhythms of poetry, the writing flowed.

By the time we completed our book, we had lost all objectivity. We were hopelessly in love with each and every set of siblings pictured. What had started out for us as an accommodation, a favor to a friend, ended as a rich emotional education about the meaning of the sibling relationship—its power and pain and enduring essence.

We hope, dear reader, as you leaf through this book that somewhere, on some page, you'll find yourself and your brother or sister, and rediscover the meaning you have for each other.

To our brothers and sisters around the world.
Let us be family for each other.

Prologue

BROTHERS AND SISTERS, AFTER ALL

Mother . . . Father . . . Child
A tight little universe
of nurturers and nurtured
of dreamers and the dream come true.
A circle of love.

Why break it?
Why another child?
(or two or three or more)
Only for the moment, to make the circle wider.
More warmth. More joy.

Brothers and sisters laughing and loving
Shaping their childhood from a hundred happy happenings
Confidants and friends
A Bulwark. Strong and safe together
in a cold, indifferent world.
There for each other when we no longer are.
Sweet vision of sibling harmony!

You'll see, you'll love the baby.
It will be your baby, too.

No!

It's here!
Born.
Who is this stranger?
What is a "brother"?
What is a "sister"?
A ROBBER
of time for only two
A THIEF
of arms and laps
A STEALER
of songs and stories and smiles for you alone.

Go away, stranger.
Get lost and never be found.
Not ever!

But if it has to stay, then what's the way?

BE IT!
Wet your bed
suck your thumb
and cry, cry, cry.
Or
Hit it. Kiss it. Feed it. Bite it. Tease it. Play with it.

Play with it?
Peek-a-boo
Mush in the mud
Push on the swing
Pull in the wagon
It's my turn, crybaby.

Mother is having another?
Not again!

WHY!!
Even less for us now.

Oh well . . . let's play.
Wrestle and tumble
Hide-and-Go-Seek
Race down the hill
I won!

Marbles
Checkers
Pick-Up Sticks
Crazy-Eights . . . Gin Rummy . . . War
Cheater! Liar! Get out of my room!

Let's go to the beach
Skate on the pond
Hang out in the street
We're having a party.
No, you can't come. My friends don't want you.

When did he grow taller
than me?
When did she get prettier
than me?
He's so smart. Mom likes him best.
She's so sweet. Daddy's little darling.
They're disgusting!

But
you can tell her private things
and she won't tell
And he will help you with your math
And she defends you when Dad yells

And he'll lend his camera if you're "careful."
And she listens when you give advice
And he protects you from the bully on the block.

Scattered now
Busy now
Different schools, different paths.
A letter . . . now and then
A phone call . . . now and then.

Back home for the holidays
Hugs and Happiness.
You look terrific!
When did you cut your hair?
When did you grow a beard?
The table is beautiful.
Everything smells so good.
Home, home at last
Each in his own accustomed chair.

You still eat like a pig . . .
only kidding.
You still act like a jerk . . .
only kidding.

Children, children!

So you dropped math. That figures.
You think you know me, don't you?
He's only showing off.
As usual.

Now children, that's enough!

Two people sitting in each sibling seat
The adult that is

The child that was
Locked into the past.
When will we see each other as we are?
As we are striving to become?

Sorry if I hurt you.
I guess I was thinking how you always used to . . .
But that's because you always used to . . .
I never did.
You did too.
Well, if I did, it was because I felt . . .
I didn't know that.
Well now you do.
Oh.

Grown up at last!
Rivalries behind us. No need to compete.
Homes of our own
Work of our own
Loves of our own.
My brother, the teacher, makes less money.
My sister, the nurse, has more children.
My children are smarter than her children.
My house is bigger than his house.

What do we do about Mom?
Can't put her in a nursing home.
She'd never go.
I'd never let her.
Maybe you could take her.
Why me?
You're her favorite.
I had her for a month this summer.
But I'm the one who sees her every day.

Our children are grown.
Our parents are gone.

We remain.
My brother, my sister, myself.

So strange. He turns his graying head and laughs
and there's the boy again.
She gestures with a wrinkled hand
and there's the girl again.
Do you remember when . . .
Oh yes, oh yes! Do you remember when . . . ?

My brother, my sister, myself.
You went to the doctor?
What did he say?
Another opinion?
I'm here if you need me.

Comforters for our todays
Guardians of memories
Keeping our youth and yesterdays alive
Comrades with one history.

No one cares
who is better
who is worse
who has more
who has less.
Content in our connectedness
we are brothers and sisters
after all.

BETWEEN
BROTHERS & SISTERS

GESTATION

A time of magic and mystery
A life that never was before
is growing . . . growing
soon to make its presence known.

The family is on the brink of change
its very structure
about to come apart
and be reordered.

Mother wonders and worries:
How will I manage with two?
Both of them needing me
Both of them calling me
Who will I go to first?

Father wonders and worries:
Will we have the money?
Will we have the room?
Will we have the time?
Will they get along?

Child wonders and worries:
Why are they having it?
Because I'm not good enough?
Once it gets born
will they love me as much?

A new baby is coming! You can hear it . . .

but you can't see it.

The baby will be <u>this</u> big!

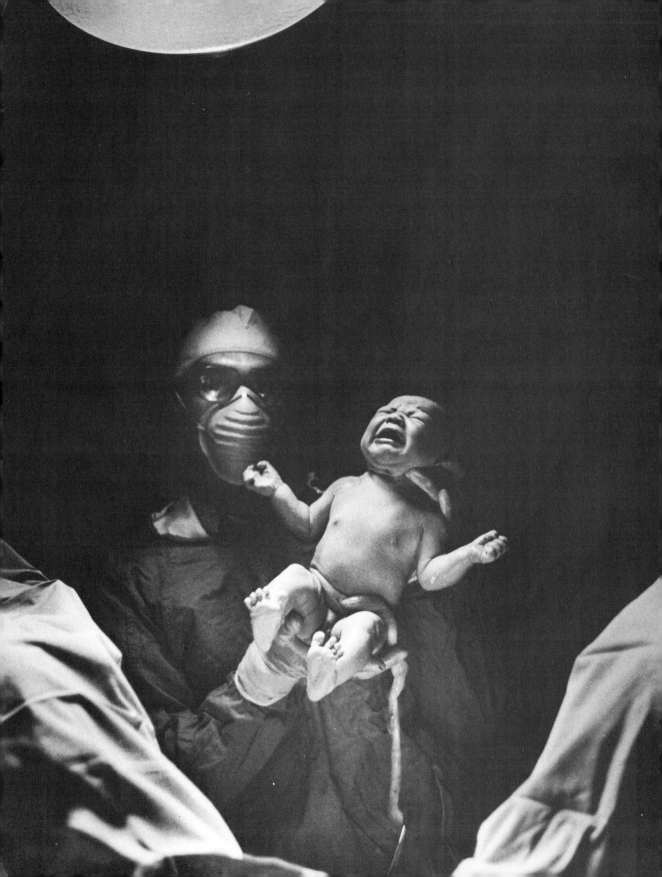

It's so little.

ADJUSTMENT

After the excitement and the presents and the congratulations
Reality sets in.
The daily business of living with
a squalling, spitting, wetting, helpless newborn
who requires round-the-clock care.
It must be watched over, fed, burped, bathed,
powdered, dressed, and changed . . .
endlessly.

There are new sounds in the house.
After . . .
As soon as . . .
Be patient . . .
Wait . . .

After I feed him, I'll read you a story.
As soon as I change her, I'll get you your juice.
Try to be patient. I'll be with you soon.
I'm bathing the baby. You'll just have to wait.

The tiny intruder dominates the day.
Its needs take precedence over everything.
And everyone.
And the older child wonders
How come the baby is so important?
How come I'm not anymore?
Do I still belong?
Where do I fit in?

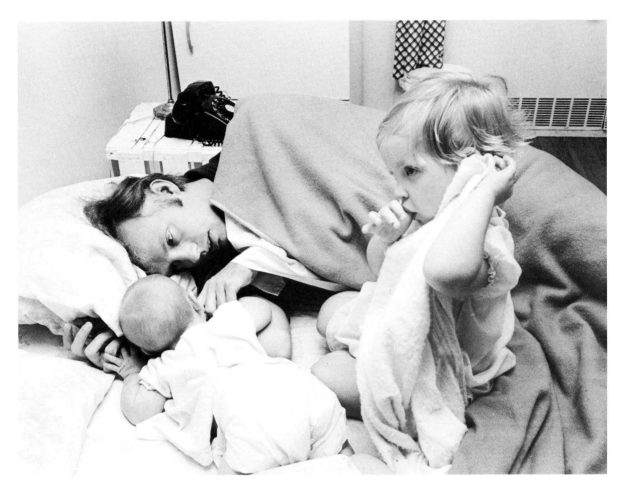

He's forgotten all about me.

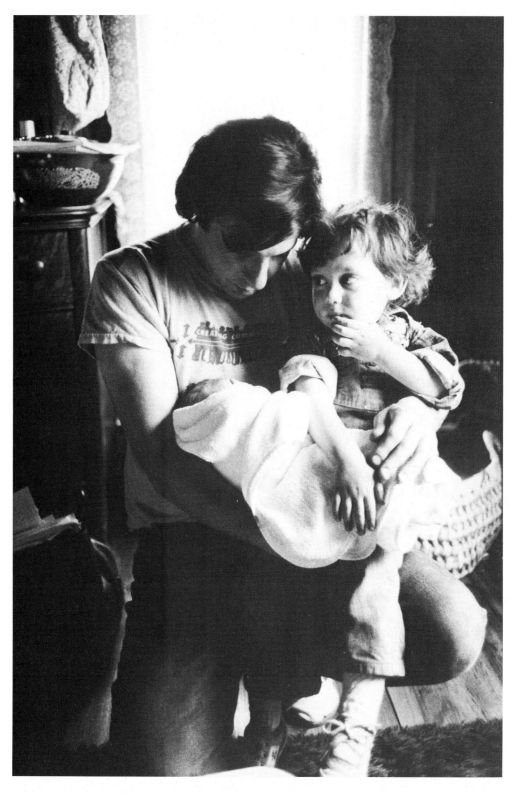

He only looks at her.

Me! Hold me!

This is where I belong.

Her arms are big enough to hold us all.

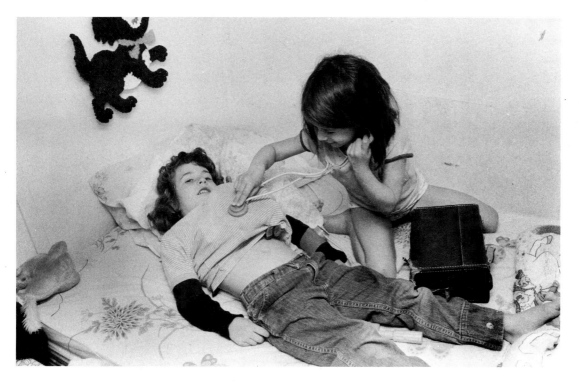

I'm having a baby, too.

My baby needs to be nursed.

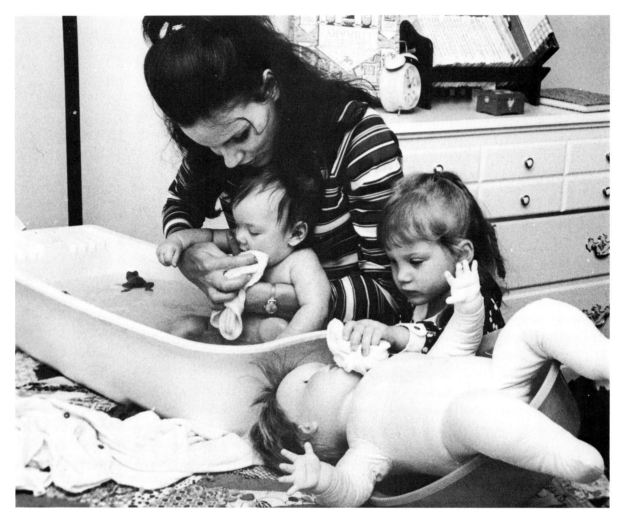

My baby keeps me busy.

BEING OLDEST (THE GOOD PART)

OLDEST means
being bigger and smarter
because older brothers and sisters
can do a lot of things a baby can't
like hop and sing and talk in sentences
and say the alphabet from A to Z.

Oh the pleasure of being two steps ahead!
Superior
Of knowing and showing
an adoring admirer
a world full of wonders.
Pebbles and puddles
and ladybugs and creeping caterpillars
and how to blow the fluffy stuff off a dandelion
and watch it disappear into the air.

The older child
once a helpless infant
now transformed
into teacher, mentor, leader
BOSS

Being oldest means being in charge!

When babies are little, there's not much you can do with them.

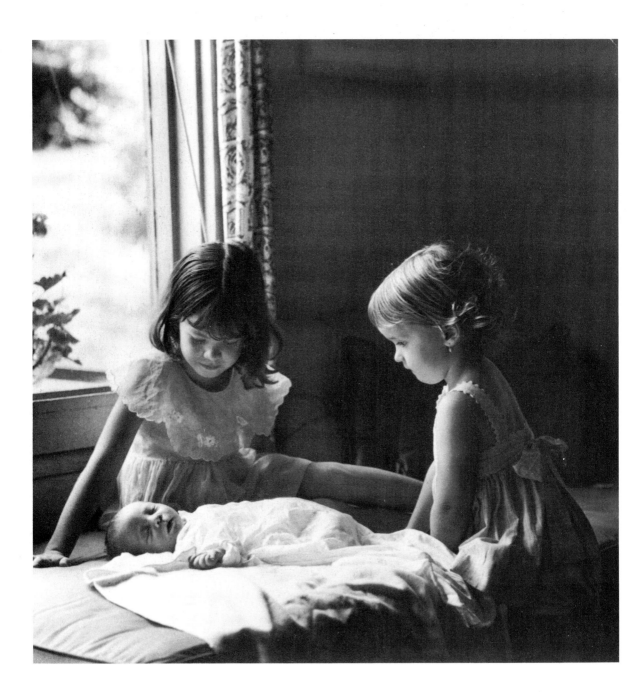

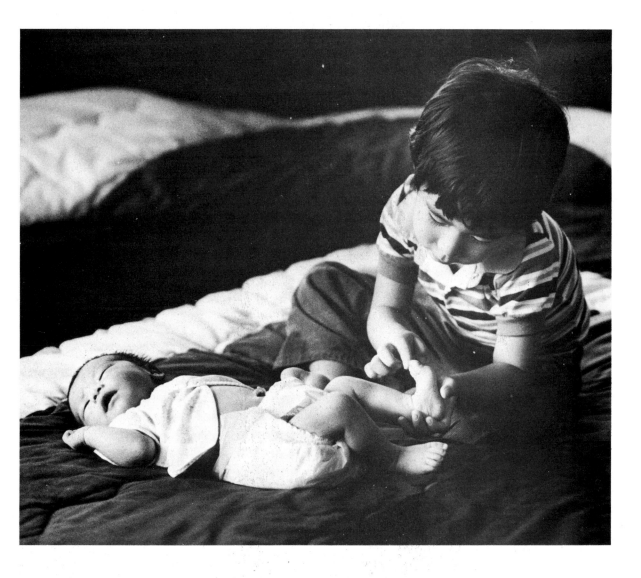

But when they get bigger you can hold them

or put them in a box

and have fun with them.

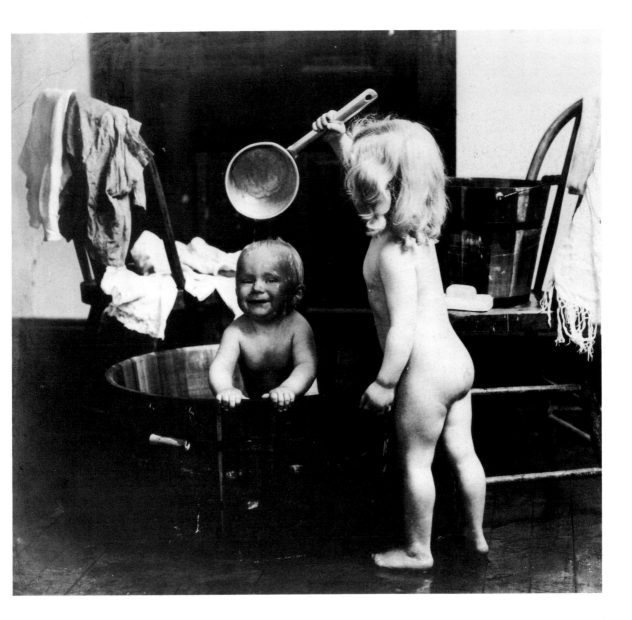

You can even watch TV together.

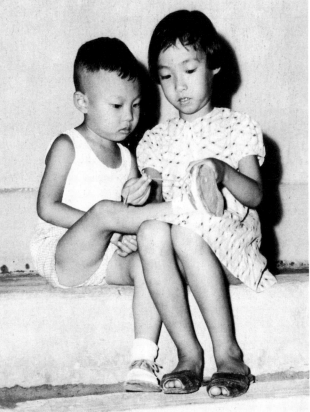

and teach them things

like how to read

or how to say A-P-P-L-E

or "hello" to Grandma

and what to watch for when you cross the street.

BEING OLDEST (THE BAD PART)

OLDEST means
giving up
tricycles and teddy bears and outgrown clothes
and half a room
and being told
You have to learn to share.

OLDEST means
building the tallest block tower in the world
and seeing it smashed to the ground
by a poke from a pest.

OLDEST means
being blamed.
The baby is crying.
What did you do?
You must have done something.
Just leave her alone.

OLDEST means
never acting silly anymore
because grown-ups disapprove
but they love it when the baby acts that way.

OLDEST means
never going anywhere without
someone tagging along
and always being imitated
by a little copycat.

OLDEST means hearing
Let the baby have it.
You can find something else to play with.
We expect you to set an example.
Now stop that crying and act your age.

Being oldest can feel very unfair.

Little brothers and sisters can be a pain in the neck.

They show off like they're so cute.

They try to spoil your birthday.

They can make you so mad!

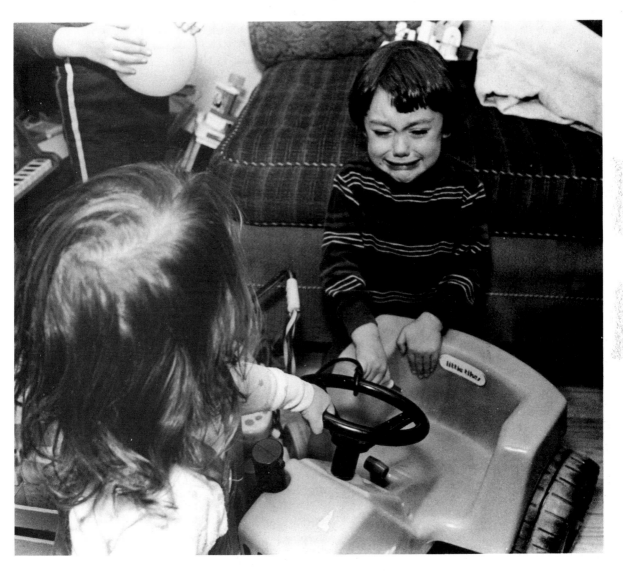

Especially when they cry because you want your toy back.

Sometimes it's fun to see them cry.

Younger brothers and sisters mean more work

and less time for play.

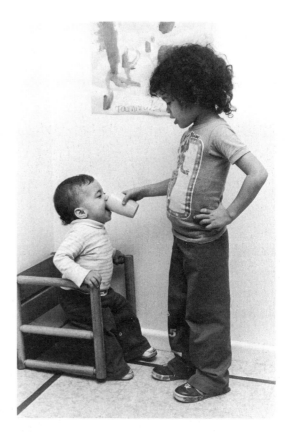

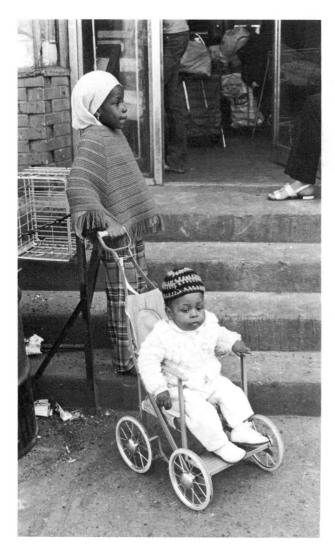

You have to take them with you . . .

wherever you go.

And they can be heavy.

But sometimes you hardly notice they're there.

YOUNGEST

Protected . . . Adored . . . Indulged.
A privileged character
in the family drama
or so you'd think.

But there's more to it than that.
It's being last
and running hard behind
and never catching up.
And being called "the baby"
no matter how big you become.
And getting pushed around
and pushing back with all your might
and finding out
it does no good.
And watching the older kids in the family
do things and go places
and being told
Not you.
Not now.
Not yet.
Maybe next year.

But then again
having a big brother or sister
can be like having
a hero in the house.
Someone to look up to
A doer of daring deeds
A bold brave
who'll scout the territory ahead

and tell you when to stay behind
and when it's safe to go.

A personal interpreter
who's privy to the secrets of the grown-up world
and translates all the double talk
and tells you what it means
like *in the family way*
and *passed away*
and why poor Aunt Alice
was *put away*.

But best of all
being youngest means
you get extra time.
Time to watch your sister and brother
fight with Mom
challenge Dad
break new ground
make mistakes
and grow up.

And while you watch
what's happening to them
you can think about
what *you* want to do
how *you* want to do it
who *you* want to be.

My big brother is always teasing me.

My sister is very bossy. She makes me try things even if I'm scared.

Every time I ask to borrow something she says, "Well I don't know . . ."

I'm glad I have an older brother.

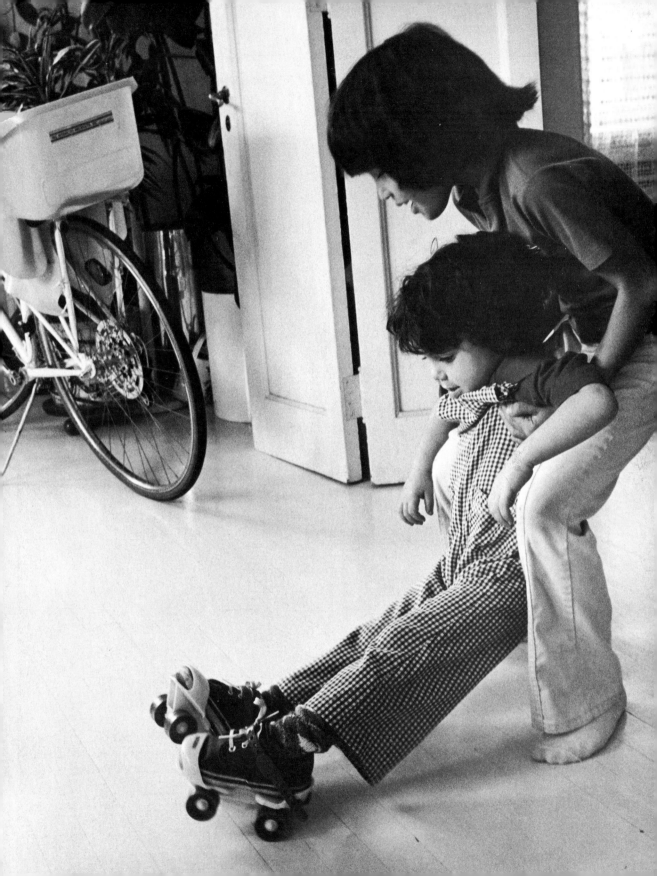

It's great to have a big sister!

I have a lot of different feelings about my sister.

The best part
of having a brother or sister
is never being alone.

When your friend says
I can't come over
and Mom says
I'm busy
and Dad says
I'm paying bills
and all your toys
are boring and babyish
and there's no school
and nothing to do
nothing at all . . .

There's always someone around
to play with
pretend with
invent with
Someone who'll do things with you
that are fun
or forbidden
or a little dangerous.

Grown-ups always ask
Why do you two fight all the time?

For any reason
or no reason.

ANY REASON could be
she calls you "fatso"
he reads your diary
she hogs the bathroom
he cheats at checkers
she takes your T-shirt
he breaks your record
she gives a play punch
it's *not* a play punch.

NO REASON could be
you were teased at the bus stop
fell on the playground
were sent to the office
left homework at home
were scolded by mother
frowned on by father
for not being like brother
and the kids on the block said,
You can't be on our team and
no one has time to listen to your troubles.
Then you have to
hit your brother
or kick your sister
'cause they're the only ones
it's safe to let it out on
especially if
they're smaller than you.

Play fights can be fun!

Sometimes what starts out as a play fight

turns into a real fight!

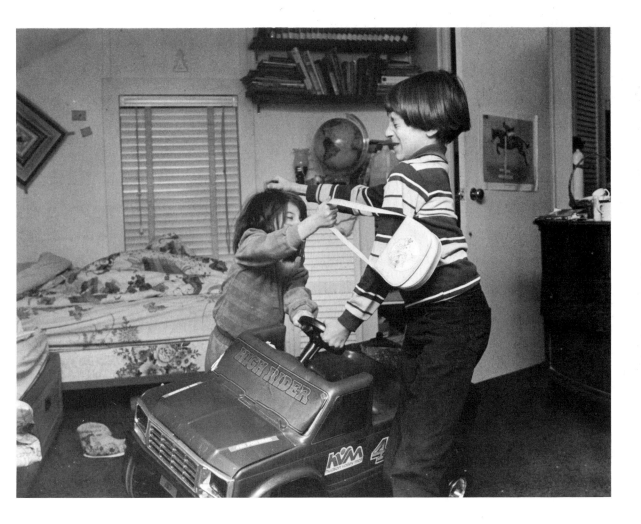

If your Dad catches you, he stops you

and then you both get in trouble.

The thing about fighting
with your brother and sister is
you don't stay mad forever.

And even though
you may hit each other
nobody else better try.

And even though
you call each other bad names
nobody else better say anything bad.

Deep inside you know
when trouble comes
and there's no one else to turn to
you can call on each other
and count on each other
to care for each other
because each other
is all you have.

When no one else wants us, we have each other.

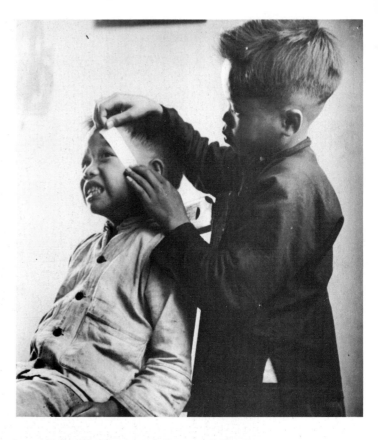

It's good to have someone who will
help you when you're hurt

and keep you from harm.

We mourn together for the brother we lost.

I weep with joy for the brother I found.

Some brothers and sisters
are worlds apart
in taste and temperament.
The lover of Mozart
cannot comprehend
how his sibling can listen to Rock.
The one who likes people
cannot understand
why his brother is happy alone.

Then there are those
whose passion is one.
Who thrill to the very same thing.
From the earliest years
they work as a team
no problem too large
no detail too small
cheering each other on
bucking each other up
fueling each other's dreams.

We both like construction. When we grow up we're going to build a house.

We like to make things that go.

We're starting our own business. Maybe someday we'll have a store.

We both love sports.

People say if we keep practicing we could have our own band one day.

We make up our own songs.

We like to clown around and make people laugh.

Sometimes we talk about how we'll help our country when we grow up.

WHAT MAKES US SIBLINGS?

Nurtured in the same dark womb
sired by one father
held close by one mother
reared under the same roof
steeped in the same traditions
sung the same songs,
we share a double line of ancestors
that reaches back to the beginning of time.

Each, part of the past
part of father
part of mother
part of each other.

Echoes of each other's being.
Whose eyes are those that look like mine?
Whose smile reminds me of my own?
Whose thoughts come through with just a glance?
Who knows me as no others do?
Who in the whole wide world is most like me
yet not like me at all?

My sibling.

People say you can tell we're sisters

They seem to know we're brothers.

Even a sister and brother can look like each other.

Mother dresses us alike so people will know we're sisters.

We were born within minutes of each other.

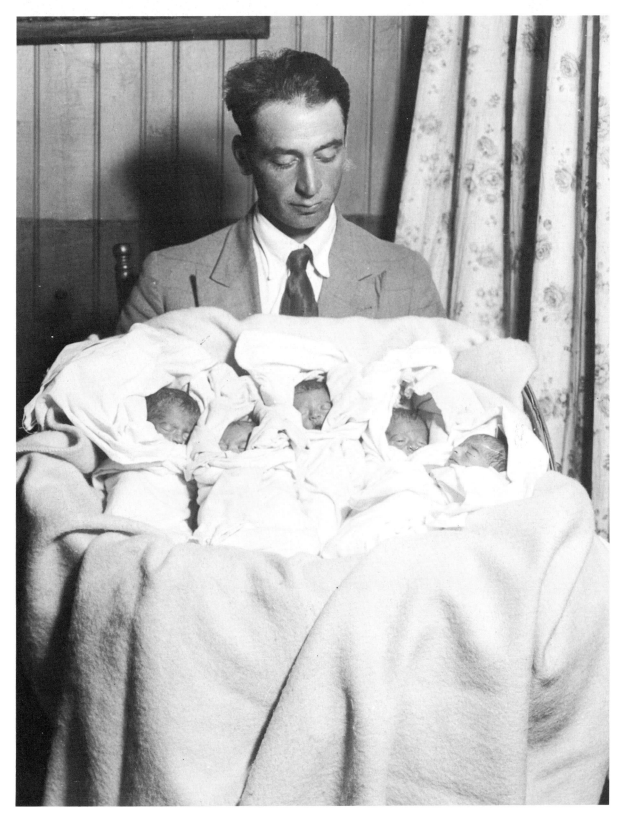

We were born a generation apart.

We're all girls.
But finally . . .

A boy!

Mom's still trying for a girl.

OTHER SIBLINGS

Half
Step
Adopted
Foster
How do these siblings come to be?
Each has a different history.

If mother marries again
and has a baby boy
you get to have a half brother.

If father marries again
and his new wife already has a child
you get to have a stepbrother or a stepsister.

If a mother knows she can't give her baby girl
the kind of care she deserves
the mother might decide
her baby is better off
with *your* mother
and then you get to have an adopted sister.

And sometimes parents become very ill
or have other bad troubles
and their little boy is placed in your home
until their troubles are over
and then you get to have a foster brother.

These siblings don't come the regular route.
Some connect with the family quickly.

From the moment they arrive, they belong
are part of the whole.
Others take time
time for you to feel at home with them
and they with you.
There's much that's unfamiliar.
Irritating.

But after you live with them
play with them
eat with them
sleep with them
fight with them
they become
your brothers and sisters.

Our stepmother is having a baby.

We may not look like brothers and sisters . . .

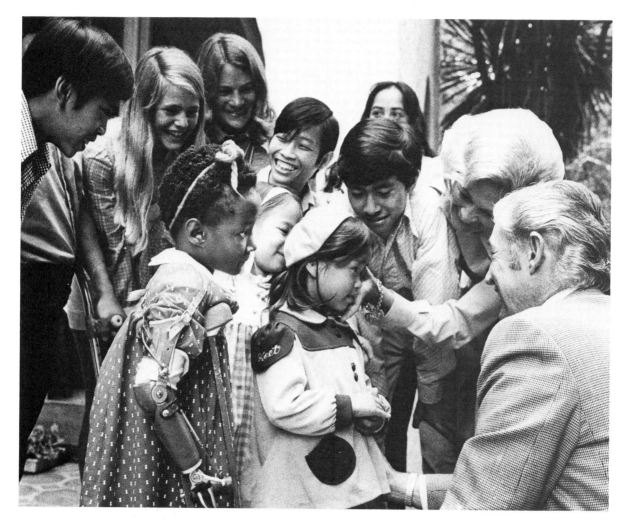

but we are!

We don't look like our parents,

but they are our parents.

Our mother and father don't look like each other . . .

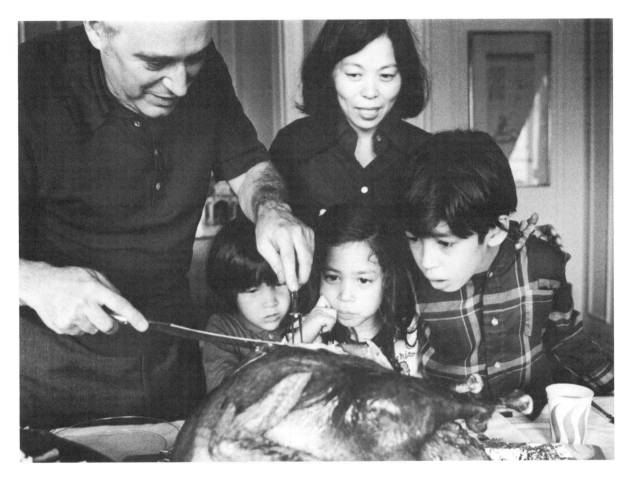

but we do.

Nothing's the same anymore.
The skinny kid who cried a lot
now has big broad shoulders.
The little girl who played with dolls
now reads Shakespeare's sonnets.

Nothing's the same anymore.
We used to lie awake at night
trading jokes and scary stories
and talk about what to wear for Halloween
and what we wanted for Christmas.
Now our late-night conversations
turn to far more sober subjects
college, careers and the greenhouse effect
and we probe the mysteries of the opposite sex.

Nothing's the same anymore.
My brother and I were always at odds
Now we like being together.
My sister and I used to be close
Now there's a chasm between us.
Nothing's the same anymore.

She always tries to put me down.

And I hate it when she tattles on me and Mom says, "She did <u>what!!</u>"

We're very different people. What he thinks is funny, I don't.

Sometimes he makes me so angry!

We never got along and still don't.

We always got along and still do.

It's fun to hang out together.

It's good to have someone to help you with decisions . . .

someone to confide in.

Someone you can talk to . . .

heart to heart.

So fast.
It's all going by
so fast.
It used to be that our summers never ended
and our birthdays never came
and everything we dreamed of doing
or being
was scheduled for
the
far
and
distant
future.

Now our summers go by
in a moment.
And our birthdays come 'round
in a flash.
And the future is hard upon us
and all the things
we wondered about
and worried about
and looked forward to
and feared
are suddenly
HERE.

Now we have children of our own . . .

who call our mother, "Grandma."

Our lives are very different now.
We each have new priorities.
Our mates, our kids, our homes, our work
all make their claims upon our time
and challenge us at every turn.

It's hard to get together now.
But when we do
we're glad we did.
Somehow we fall into
an old familiar mode
a reassuring rhythm
that restores us
and reminds us
that some things
remain the same.

It doesn't matter what we do. It's being together that counts.

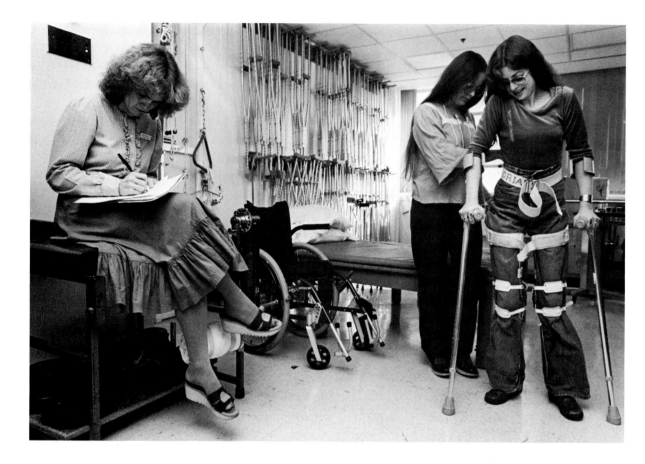

It's good to have someone close who'll give you support when you need it.

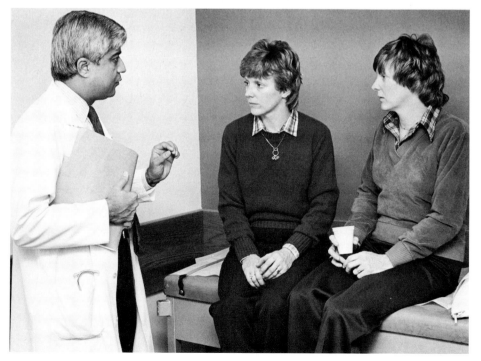

Someone who'll share the good times

and the bad.

We may live far apart, but when we get together there's no distance between us.

We need each other in new ways now.
To parent our parents
to give each other strength
as they decline
to fill the gap of friends
who move away or die
to face the last uncertain years
together.
We need each other in new ways now.

But what if there's been
bitterness between us
And things were said or done
that left deep wounds?
Shall we say, *Goodbye.*
It's finished. Over.
Or should we try to make repairs
and start again?

Could you forgive me
for the hurts that I've inflicted?
Could I forgive you
for the words you hurled my way?
Could we speak the truth
and really hear each other
and wash away the hurt
with healing tears?

Or should we let lie
old, long-buried feelings
and say *what's in the past
is in the past*
and concentrate on what is good between us
however little
whatever little
and be glad
for that little.
We need each other in new ways now.

*We become more precious to each other
with every passing year.*

We laugh the easy laughter . . .

of people who have shared a lifetime.

There's no need to talk. We know each other's thoughts.

We know each other's ways.

He still fusses over me.

We still like to share dessert.

And we still work together, just as we did when we were young.

Once a year we visit Mama and Papa's grave

and take comfort in each other.

Our bodies are old now
But, oh, our memories . . .
Our memories are young
and alive!

Photo Credits